Faithful Servant Series
Meditations for Lay Readers

Suzanne E. Hunger
Christopher L. Webber, Series Editor

D1566163

MOREHOUSE PUBLISHING

Copyright © 1999 by Suzanne Hunger

Morehouse Publishing
P.O. Box 1321
Harrisburg, PA 17105
Morehouse Publishing is a division of The Morehouse Group.

Unless otherwise noted, the Scripture quotations contained herein are from the New Revised Standard Version Bible, copyright © 1989 by the Division of Christian Education of the National Council of the Churches of Christ in the U.S.A. Used by permission. All rights reserved.

Library of Congress Cataloging-in-Publication Data

Hunger, Suzanne E.
    Meditations for lay readers / by Suzanne E. Hunger.
        p.   cm. — (Faithful servant series)
    Includes bibliographical references.
    ISBN 0-8192-1771-9 (pbk.)
    1. Lay readers — Episcopal Church — Prayer-books and devotions — English. I. Title. II. Series.
BX5967.5.H86 1999
242'.69 — dc21
                        98-55385
                        CIP

Passages marked BCP are from The Book of Common Prayer.

Printed in the United States of America

Cover design by Corey Kent

Contents

"You Were Chosen"

Were you chosen to read this book? Perhaps it was given to you in a public ceremony or maybe it was handed to you with a quiet "you might like to look at this." Maybe, on the other hand, it reached out to you in a bookstore and said, "Buy me!" Many books choose us in such ways and this book is likelier to have done so than most. But however this book came to you, it almost certainly happened because you have also been chosen for a ministry in the church or for church membership. Perhaps you hadn't considered this as being chosen; you thought you decided for yourself. But no, you were chosen. God acted first, and now you are where you are because God took that initiative.

God acts first—the Bible is very clear about that and God acts to choose us because God loves us. And who is this God who seeks us in so many ways, who calls us from our familiar and comfortable places and moves us into new parishes and new roles? Christians have been seeking answers to that question for a long time.

Part of the answer can be found within the church. We come to know God better by serving as church members and in church ministries. God is present with us and in others all around us as we worship and serve. But there is always more, and God never forces a way into our hearts. Rather, God waits for us to be quiet and open to a deeper relationship.

And that's what this book is about. This is not simply a book to read but to use, in the hope that you will set aside some time every day for prayer and the Bible—and for this book. So give yourself time not only to read but to consider, to think about, to meditate on what you have read. The writers of these short meditations have been where you are, thought about their experiences deeply, and come to know God better. Our prayer is that through their words and experience and your reflection on them, you will continue to grow in knowledge and love—and faithful service—of this loving, seeking God.

— Christopher L. Webber
    Series Editor

Introduction

"What is the ministry of the laity? The ministry of lay persons is to represent Christ and his Church; to bear witness to him wherever they may be; and, according to the gifts given them, to carry on Christ's work of reconciliation in the world; and to take their place in the life, worship, and governance of the Church" (BCP, 855).

These words from our catechism provide powerful directions to those of us who try to be faithful servants in God's church. To open oneself to formal lay ministry takes great courage and faith. But for many of us the call to serve is a persistent one, and when lived out, it brings much blessing, even as it brings challenges. This book of meditations is designed to be a companion for that journey in faith as you serve the church, using your gifts to bring the Word of God to God's people.

When I was growing up, Morning Prayer was the predominant Sunday service in my church; it had a lovely spaciousness and time for reflection. Our small rural church had Evening Prayer each Sunday as well. I remember the dark church on cold winter evenings, filled with quiet prayers for safety and peace. These beautiful services, along with Noonday Prayer and Compline, provide prayer, fellowship, and teaching, and can all be led by lay readers. This book offers insights into the spirituality of these services, as well as suggestions about what supports and sustains Christian leaders, the means of developing one's own spirituality and connectedness to God, and ways to integrate Scripture reading into one's own life. Vignettes from my experiences as a lay reader, diocesan lay administrator, lay preacher, ski instructor, and mother illustrate and illuminate these offerings. I hope they invoke for you the same feelings that were instilled in me as a child when I sat through those marvelous times of prayer and reflection.

May the meditations and prayers found here uphold and guide lay readers in the ministry of the Word. For the Word is a gift to the people of God, and its bearers are people of faith. May the words of this book minister to those who serve their church faithfully in prayer.

In Christ's name,
Amen

——— Using This Book to Your Service ———

This book, like other meditation books, may be used in a variety of ways. The following are some simple suggestions. In the last section of the book you will find fourteen prayers: one for the morning and one for the evening of each day of the week. You might use these to start and finish your day, or if you have a daily prayer schedule, you might add these to that discipline. If you do not pray regularly, these might provide you with a starting place. The prayers are written to include the principal kinds of prayer—adoration, praise, thanksgiving, penitence, oblation, intercession, and petition—and give intentional attention to lay reading.

Along with prayer, Scripture reading can be a source of support for lay readers. Because our ministry is very visible among people, we are expected to know something about the words we read and proclaim. Bible studies, formal programs like Education for Ministry (EFM), and daily reading and studying of the Bible build good foundations for lay readers' ministry. The meditations in this book offer a number of Scripture quotations that may send the reader to the Bible to look for the context or further expression of an idea. Following a thought from a meditation to the Bible and then into your life can enrich your spiritual life as well as your theological understanding of Scripture.

The Book of Common Prayer is used extensively in these meditations because for Episcopalians the prayer book is a source of information, spiritual insights, theological explanations, and challenges to be met in one's ministry. The meditations may provide you with a new way of using a prayer or section of the prayer book, or they may offer an addition to your personal discipline of prayer. You might use the meditations with prayer book citations as a means to further explore the prayer book—for example, reading Compline after a meditation on it.

Some meditations offer very practical advice on how you might handle a particular situation. Most of the meditations are written with the particular ministry of lay reading in mind. In my lay ministry I have found that keeping myself in right relation with God has had to be my main priority, so I have written from those experiences with the hope that you'll find something that will fire your flame of faith.

You may, as I often do with books of meditations, quickly read the book from cover to cover; in this way you get an overview and can then return to particular meditations for a less rushed encounter with them. You may wish to read one each day until you have read them all. Once you have found time to read them, you will want to reflect on them. Let a single meditation rest in your mind all day, and then at the end of the day write in a journal, reflecting on whether anything was different or more focused in your day because of the meditation you read. After reading one, you might want to sit for a few minutes and think about how you would have approached a similar situation or passage. You might engage in some internal dialog about the meditation. Or you might use the meditations for a lay reader study, prayer, or support group, reading a meditation or two at each meeting and following them with discussion, focusing on how God seems to be working in your life. When I read meditations slowly and thoughtfully, I find it helpful to pause and think how I might apply someone else's learnings to my life. I seek the light of God in the writing and let that illuminate my life. For it is in the sharing of our lives in God that we grow in God and help others to grow as well.

"Here I am."

(Genesis 22:1b)

"Here I am, Lord," we sing in church. "Here I am, Lord." The Harper Collins Study Bible reminds us that this is the "archetypal response of the faithful servant of God" (32). "Here I am, Lord." What faith we show when we declare ourselves to God. We don't say, "Here I am, Lord—wonderful person, great lay reader, virtuous churchgoing person." No, we like Abraham simply say, here I am with all my warts and bruises and humanity—my anger, my self-pity, my laughter, my disbelief, my belief, my hurts, my wants, and my passions. It takes great courage to answer this way when God calls. Many of us would rather run and hide behind a fig leaf so that God can not see us naked with our passions, agonies, dismay, and frailties all hanging out, exposed. But God does not ask us to hide. God invites us to share in the great existence of the "I am." God wants us to be lights visible, not hidden under a bushel basket. We are to declare boldly to the world that we are with God and in God and from God.

"Here I am" is the beginning of a way of life in response to God's call to us. When we announce "Here I am" to the Lord, we are announcing to the world that a different set of standards is now in effect for us. God doesn't ask that we get all gussied up for God or that we hide our true selves behind safe pronouncements and false piety. God asks that we stand up and be counted, that we be with God, and that we stay in the creative process of becoming all that we can be, and at the same time have faith that it is not our polished manners that God wants but our heart, our wholeness, our joy, and our humanity. God wants us "as is"— nothing more, nothing less.

*Keep them in the faith and communion of your holy Church.
LORD, hear our prayer. Teach them to love others in the power
of the Spirit. LORD, hear our prayer.*

(BCP, 305)

The ministry of lay readers begins at baptism, where we are committed to our life in Christ. From the Baptismal Covenant and the Prayers for the Candidates, we begin to see the shape of our ministry take place.

We are called to be faithful, to trust that God wills us to be co-creators with God. We are called to take the risk of loving one another into being and creativity, to take leaps of faith that reject the comforts of the status quo, the security of money and prestige. We are asked to help one another reject the ever present fig leaf, designed to keep us safe from onlookers who might condemn us if they could see beyond the covering we wear.

It is not an easy life when we answer to God in faith, but it is a life worth living, a life that honors God, a life that builds up the creation of God and does not destroy it by turning its back on love and trust. As we help one another answer "Here I am, Lord," we help ourselves learn again that these words bring us into a right relation with God, one that allows us to forgive and to be forgiven. It is a relationship that honors both the faith God has in us and the faith we have in God. Teaching and sharing with others what we have learned by living out our baptismal ministry, we proclaim the gospel in a very real way—one that upholds those we serve in faith.

A Prayer of Self-Dedication: Almighty and eternal God, so draw our hearts to thee, so guide our minds, so fill our imaginations, so control our wills, that we may be wholly thine, utterly dedicated unto thee; and then use us, we pray thee, as thou wilt, and always to thy glory and the welfare of thy people; through our LORD and Savior Jesus Christ. Amen.

(BCP, 832–833)

I suspect that many of us have a hard time with the words of this prayer. In asking for our "Here I am," and in asking for our "Yes, Lord," God doesn't ask us for something easy—for a bit of our time, talent, or treasure. God asks that our whole being be given in service to God and God's people and world. We are always free to answer no to the call from God. But once we have responded to it, we are asked to give everything we have. We are to bow our wills to that of God, to understand that God wants for us more than we can imagine for ourselves, more than we know we need. God wants us to move into relation to God. And God's models are not easy to follow. Consider the models of the prophets, who were despised in their own lands; Moses, who dealt with the complaints and whines of his people; Mary, who cried at the cross; and Jesus, who died for us and then rose again, bearing all our sins. And yet their lives were blessed in ways we can only begin to imagine.

Lay readers often hear the call to work for God's people in a very concrete way. They are to bring God's Word to the people gathered, to answer yes and take the leap into the political world of the church, to open oneself up to criticism, and to put oneself out in front, where one's warts may show. I think many of us who serve the church in a very public way, who become privy to the inner workings of the church, sometimes wish we could return and just be a person in the pew. But that is not to be: The people in the pews answer a different call from God. Lay readers answer the call to lead, officiate, and let their voice and being remind the people that the people are God's beloved.

I have felt blessed to have the voice and presence to stand in front of a group of children and lead them in an outdoor chapel, through the howling wind, in the service of Evening Prayer. Despite the wind and the squirrels (who insisted on throwing pinecones throughout the service), the children heard that God loved them. In telling them that, I was reminded of how wide and how merciful God is. God used me to reach the children; it is good and right to say yes to that. God wills that each child know that the very hairs on his or her head are counted by God. Each is counted as important and should celebrate a life worth living. If God can use me to carry that message, than I am blessed indeed.

What is the communion of saints? The communion of saints is the whole family of God, the living and the dead, those whom we love and those whom we hurt, bound together in Christ by sacrament, prayer, and praise.

(BCP, 862)

My nephew prays in the background of my phone conversation with my sister: "Dear God, please make Granmommy well and not be sick anymore." My sister automatically responds, "Amen," as do I. Somewhere this five year old has learned about the power of prayer. In this almost unobserved moment, I feel closer to this child than I ever have before. He is praying for my mother, who is sick. My friends, some of whom my mother has never met, are praying for her as well.

I check my answering machine and find an encouraging message from a friend: "I was just calling to see how your stepmom is doing. Let me know. She was in my prayers last night, and I wanted to know." My friend has never met my stepmom, yet she prays for her, joined together in the "whole family of God."

This is a miracle. In a world where we are told to stick to ourselves, to not trust strangers, to avoid being hurt, to separate ourselves from those who pose a threat, to not get involved, and to avoid lawsuits at all costs, we occasionally witness our own willingness to let God in, to ask for God's healing. When we do this, when we are willing to pray for those whom we love and for those whom we hurt, we are opening ourselves to the miracle of God's love, to the healing presence of light in our lives. In prayer, we begin to knit together the communion of saints.

I find it difficult to remain mad at someone for whom I pray. I may have hurt that person, or that person may have hurt me, but I am called by my Baptismal Covenant to be a reconciler in this world, and my first step is prayer. If in my own heart I can find room to pray for someone, then I can forgive or ask for forgiveness. Here heart and mind mingle, much as they did for the writers of the New Testament.

Much has been written about the healing power of prayer; scientific studies and doctors' anecdotes discuss the benefits of prayer. A woman facing a biopsy calls and says that the specialists could find nothing when they went to perform the procedure. There is relief in her voice, but as she talks about the people who have offered prayers of healing for her, real joy sounds with each word. She has met love face to face in the prayers of these people. She lists the ones she knows and wonders at those who prayed but whom she has never met. Prayer provides the opportunity for joining people together in community, in the communion of saints. We are bound together by our mutterings to God, by our belief in the love that will come from those prayers, and by our praise for the chance to pray for one another. In this gift of prayer, we reach out to one another across the boundaries of distrust and fear—this is a miracle. We reach out beyond the perceived safety of our own little self-world and enter into the infinite world of compassion. As part of the communion of saints, lay readers have a particular ministry: to lead the prayers and to lead the services. We are called by God to do so.

For minds to think, and hearts to love, and hands to serve, We thank you, LORD.

(BCP, 837)

When I sit on the Commission on Ministry and listen to the calls and struggles of those who believe God is calling them to seminary, or to the diocesan formation program and on to ordained ministry, I sometimes hear their unbelief. Many cannot believe that God is calling them to serve in this distinct way. Many have denied the call for years, fearing that they were not good enough or strong enough, or fearing that their lives would change too much. I don't think that these doubts happen only to those called to be ordained priests and deacons. I think that those whom God calls to be strong lay leaders in the church also struggle with them.

God's call to the laity can be as strong and unmistakable as God's call to those who will be ordained clergy. Often the call comes to us through a discerning person who is open to God's Spirit; in my case, the call to lay reading came through a priest. Sometimes the call comes through a discernment process set up by a congregation to identify the ministries and talents of its many members. One congregation that I know identified lay readers, lay preachers, musicians, administrators, and abiders (people who would abide in the Lord, sitting quietly and praying, adding their presence to the communion of God).

Most of us will struggle with the call. Will I have enough time to be parish treasurer? Do I read well enough to be a lector? I don't know anything about intercession; am I really being called to be on the prayer chain? Prayer book rubrics confuse me; can I really lead a service? Often we do not question the existence of a call; rather, we question our ability to serve, to answer the call. But we have been given minds to think, hearts to love, and hands to serve, and God will give us the strength to serve if we are willing. God knows us better than we do; he chose Moses, he chose Mary, and he chose David, his beloved king. He chose Martha and he chose Sarah, the ancestress. And he chose to call you, the lay reader, into service for God and God's people.

In serving God, call upon God the Creator, God the Son, God the Holy Spirit. In serving, call upon your fellow companions and ask for their support and faith in you. Call upon the ordained clergy to bless and teach you. Call upon the faith that God has shown in you. And know that you are answering an ancient call to worship, to heal, to reconcile, to praise, and to love.

...and you will be children of the Most High; for he is kind to the ungrateful and the wicked.

(Luke 6:35b)

"I don't need any of your old ski lessons!" the child yelled at us. "I'm not going to get in line and try that stupid exercise." Over and over this young man spit his anger out at us, glaring at us with a hatred meant to penetrate our patience. It worked; my patience was tested. We had fifteen other youngsters who wanted to learn to ski. I wanted to send this particular one far away, where I wouldn't need to deal with him, where I could forget about him. None of the other instructors wanted him around either; indeed, the week before we had finally had to send him into the lodge. But on this day, as tempers rose, I remembered what the director of skiing always says: "Make it simple. Make it positive. Make a leader out of a troublemaker if you can." And so I asked this boy if he would like to help us teach. He looked at me and the other instructor, his eyes apprehensive, not trusting. The other instructor said, "That's a great idea! You help us demonstrate the moves."

Slowly, Jerry made his way to the line of children and just as slowly he started to demonstrate the way to stop. It wasn't perfect, but we made a big deal out of it. "Great!" we yelled. "Can you do it once more?" He did it again.

We progressed up the hill, getting him to help us demonstrate how to use a ski lift, how to turn, and how to get up from falls. Once we even caught him helping another student up from the snow. After that set of lessons, we didn't see him until right before he and the other children were going home. He came up to us and said, "I've been looking for you, Coach. You two are great. Here, have a Skittle." With those two pieces of candy all was forgiven and forgotten. It was a moment made sacred.

We are called to be kind and merciful, even before the forgiveness and the forgetting. We are to reach out to the child who is trying his hardest to be unreachable. In our congregations there are often people like my student, people whose anger is explosive and who aim to destroy the community we are trying to build. These people, in their self-destructive hatred, can change the very tenor of a service, meeting, or prayer group. We are nonetheless called to be kind to them. As a lay reader coping with these people, I have tried to remember the ski director's advice: "Make it simple. Make it positive." And I have tried to find ministries for these people where they can hear the love of God.

Whoever becomes humble like this child is the greatest in the kingdom of heaven; Whoever welcomes one such child in my name welcomes me.

(Matthew 18:4–5)

I am skiing down the hill backward, holding the ski tips of a child who doesn't have the motor development to hold them together on his own. He keeps up a constant conversation about his hobbies, dinosaurs, running, baseball. His gentle speech impediment doesn't keep me from hearing the joy in his voice. I tire. Another instructor takes over. We are skiing this child into a world of freedom, one in which we move down the slope with a grace he can feel. Our movements are smooth; there is none of the jerkiness of his walking. At each new turn there is laughter. We hear the squirrels call to us. We stop and answer them, delighted that they have come to see us. At each turn we look for them. Now the other instructor tires; the snow is slow and sticky today. I move in to take hold of the skis and say that I am sorry that we have to keep stopping. The young boy replies, "I've got many patience."

How many times a day do I wish for patience. But I don't have the humility of this child, the sense that the world is wonderful despite the pain, the sense that I have time to stop and just be. The other instructor and I ended this ski day with tired and cramped muscles. Someone asked us if it was worth it. We smiled, nodded, and said, "Yes, it was worth it." To be filled with the grace and light of Christ in our presence is always worth it. Sometimes those of us who have specific ministries in our churches find the presence of Christ in those we serve outside of the church, and we are reminded of the great love God has for all people.

The Word of the LORD. Thanks be to God.

Often lay readers start out as lectors, reading from the lectionary. I didn't have much formal preparation for being a lector or a lay reader: no classes, no instruction on voice, no thorough study of the prayer book and its rubrics. In fact, my calling began innocently enough; I was asked to read the lessons one Sunday, and so I did. Then I began preparing for those Sunday readings by reading them to myself the night before, which meant I had to figure out the lectionary. I began to read more and more frequently at church, using the lessons I had learned as a teacher to project my voice, read slowly, let the rhythms of the Scripture ring true. I practiced every Saturday night, learning to read with some drama and flair.

Over time, as I went to the lectern to read, I found out a marvelous thing: I was not alone. Although the voice was mine, there was a much bigger presence in those words than I alone could give them. I began opening myself up to this presence, praying that God would enter into the words I spoke and carry them into the hearts of those present. Often

I felt my grandfather, a Presbyterian minister, with me. There was a communion in this reading that I had never imagined. I watched members of the congregation as some of these words reached them in a new way; I watched their eyes open in the acknowledgment that something had made sense to them. This deep sharing of the Word moved me often. I felt enveloped in God's love and a closeness to those I served—all of this in a way I never expected. God certainly works through those of us who least expect it. How welcome that work is to me now, and how strange it felt those first few times, when I knew the Holy Spirit empowered my reading.

*Their sound has gone out into all lands, and their message to the
ends of the world.*

(Psalm 19:4; BCP, 78)

After many weeks of being a lector, I was asked by the priest if I would
lead Morning Prayer along with another woman. I agreed, knowing
that I went into it with a deep respect and love for Morning Prayer. It
had been my favorite service as a child and, even though the prayer
book had changed some since then, the subtle cadence of the service
was still in my mind and heart. In preparation for the service, the
woman and I went over the prayers and readings for the day, talked
about where the music would come in, found the collect, and generally
had a quick course in Morning Prayer. That was my preparation for
being a lay reader. Thank goodness for the organist, who helped me to
keep my place, who knew where each piece fit even if I didn't. Since that
service, and after having been licensed by the bishop, I have read
Morning and Evening Prayer to groups ranging from two to sixty or
more. Each time, I wonder at the presence of God, which is made so
strong in the reading of those words.

Gradually I have become better at leading the service. I make it a point to study the styles of priests, deacons, and lay readers as they officiate at services, and I have adapted some of what works for them into my own personal style. Certainly those whom I admire seem to move through the service without effort. They come prepared, but they also come ready to adapt to whatever may happen. An ability to use humor helps as well. At camp we had forgotten to light the altar candles for the Eucharist; suddenly realizing this, the priest turned to the children and said, "This being Thursday, we will light the candles after the gospel reading." And he proceeded to do so. Our candles were lit, our sense of community enlarged, and it was okay. Being prepared and flexible are two keys to successfully leading a service.

Many of the churches I visit are noisy as people greet each other and chat in the pews before the service. Gone is the quiet time imposed in some churches. One priest, whose Easter service I attended, dealt with this chatty beginning in a wonderful, affirming way. He walked down to the front of the church, greeted us all with "Good Morning," and then invited us into silent prayer, praising God for the day and being thankful for God's presence among us. As we prayed in silence, the priest walked to the back of the church and waited a bit. Then the music started and the procession began. I learned much by observing this tactful way of allowing silence to move into our hearts and minds, so that in the stillness we would feel refreshed and ready to begin the service. It is one of the strategies I will use when it seems appropriate.

Let the words of my mouth and the meditation of my heart be acceptable in your sight, O LORD, my strength and my redeemer.
(Psalm 19:14; BCP, 78)

To each ministry one must bring a certain amount of discipline. Much of the discipline involved in being a lay reader is that of structuring a prayer or worship life that enables him or her to grow in God's love and to face the theological, spiritual, and physical challenges of the ministry.

Reading books on theology, those that mesh well with my own theology and those that challenge it, helps me to understand why our prayer services offer what they do and to respond to people's questions. For inevitably, once you lead a service you are apt to have coffee-hour questions posed to you.

Reading books about how people integrate prayer, rules of life, and meditation into their lives helps me to determine what might be missing in mine as well as what I am doing well. Through studying I have learned how to create a prayer corner, how to pray in a very deliberate way while on a walk, and how to use books of meditations in many ways. In doing these things, I allow spiritual growth to occur, and I model for others ways in which we can weave God into our life beyond the Sunday service. I find that having a formal or informal spiritual director helps. I have several close and trusted friends with whom I can discuss my own spiritual journey. I involve myself in a circle of friends that shares books on spirituality and theology and then gathers to discuss them. All of these increase my understanding of the strength and love of God.

I have asthma, so my physical health and ability to project my voice without running out of air are crucial to my lay reading. I seek the help of a physician and exercise in order to keep my lungs functioning well. In the winter I ski several times a week; the rest of the year I walk. These activities are a part of my prayer and writing discipline as well as a way to stay physically fit.

I have discovered that my lay reading and sermons mean more to me and others when I am clearly open to the inspiration of God; here is my strength, and I stay open to it through a disciplined life.

In the beginning was the Word, and the Word was with God, and the Word was God.

(John 1:1)

The words offered in Morning and Evening Prayer provide an understanding of an ordered universe, one made from chaos and loved into being. As we read the words and lead the service, we are reminding the people that they are loved into being. We offer words of grace, love, community, penitence, and forgiveness. We remind them that the Word has walked among us, that the Word is with us, and that God so loves us that God's Son entered this journey with us. To each person in the congregation we offer the reminder that no one is alone, that no one is without grace, and that we are God's people.

To be the bearer of that Word, each of us, like Mary, must say yes to God. Yes, I will be open. Yes, I will listen. Yes, I will stand before the congregation and let you speak through me to your people. For me, it takes a still quiet time of reading and reflection before each service so that I can say that yes with joy and understanding.

While my formal preparation for lay reading has been little, my personal preparation has been very deliberate. The night before I am to read Evening or Morning Prayer, I read through the lessons for the service, read the collect, and look for the common thread that runs through the day's readings. When I don't have to write a sermon, I often pretend I have to write one anyway. I find that understanding the readings in light of the gospel and the place in the liturgical year helps me to open myself to what God wants me to hear in the service. If I am to feed God's people in the service, I need to let myself be fed, and so I must be open, receptive, and fluid, allowing the grace of God to be present to me in the words. If I have studied them in a quiet manner before the service, something wonderful happens during the service. My understanding grows—not so much an intellectual understanding but a heart understanding. I grow in the Spirit, and I believe that as I grow in the Spirit so do the people I serve. As the Word, which is God's Spirit, moves among us, we are reminded that we are continually loved into being.

...when two or three are gathered together in his Name you will be in the midst of them.

(BCP, 126)

It certainly was intimate: Five of us sat at a round table, bundled in our sweatshirts and looking longingly at the wood stove, which sent out more smoke than heat on this damp, cold June morning. Summer camp had not yet started, but the core staff was gathered for Morning Prayer. Into this group came some of the fears that often creep into services where there are only a few gathered. Many people find the closeness of a small group and the inability to fade into the background intimidating, especially if they are to lead the service or a part of it.

Often the setting for these small groups can be intimidating as well. A hospital room or the recreation room of a nursing home can evoke those fears we may have of being sick, growing old, or dying. Into these small groups and settings lay readers can bring the peace of Christ's love, but it takes some forethought and planning, and dwelling in Christ's love to alleviate your fears as well as those of the body gathered.

I learned much in my camp experience about creating an atmosphere in which the smallness of a group becomes a strength and not a threat.

As we settled into the cold morning, our day brightened by the smell of baking muffins, I reminded the staff that in the early church the small house church was the norm, and that God is as pleased with the small group as with the large group. Before the service began, we went over some of the rubrics so that each person became comfortable with the pattern of Morning Prayer. The night before I had assigned readings to the staff so that they had time to study the lessons and the psalms. My hope was that they would not be embarrassed to read if they had been through the lessons ahead of time. We discussed a couple of pronunciations and looked over the chosen canticles so that everyone knew which we would use. Had this been a hospital room or chapel, I would have chosen, where appropriate, to shorten the service, and I would have shared those changes with people ahead of time. People often don't like the unfamiliar; so my goal as lay reader is to create a familiarity with the service and then to move us into a strong connection with each other and with God, that Christ's love can come through even the most informal reading of a service.

We didn't have a homily that cold morning, but we did talk about the beauty of the lake as the fog began lifting. We talked about the Holy Spirit's presence among us as we prepared for the campers. We offered our intercessions as well, working in our hopes and expectations for the coming summer. The informality of the setting and the inherent structure of Morning Prayer allowed us to play with the service, a play that ultimately calmed most of our fears and brought a deep appreciation of the service. One of the great learnings of my time as a lay reader has been that our love acted out as play can lift our hearts to God and can bring peace to a setting.

Give us grace, O LORD, to answer readily the call of our Savior Jesus Christ and proclaim to all people the Good News of his salvation.

(BCP, 215)

As Christians, we are called to proclaim the Good News; as lay readers, we may be asked to proclaim the Good News in the form of a sermon or homily. Formal preaching demands a certain amount of preparation, but central to that must be the sharing of God's story and of ours.

To be sure, sermons often present the church's teachings, and they demonstrate how we might live our lives. But at their very center, sermons need to tell the story of God in a way that causes it to become our story—so that our hearts mingle with the heart of God, our wisdom becomes the wisdom of God, and our wills become the will of God. Central to this telling is the gospel message that God loves us, that we are to love God, each other, and ourselves, and that Christ frees us from death. In the telling, we remind people that Jesus, the Good News incarnate, turned our world upside down with his radical views. How do we get people to hear this Good News with its challenges to our moral, ethical, and social standards? How do we get people to listen to the story that will pull them from the perceived safety of money, prestige, and popularity?

We share our stories.

Those of us who have tried to pay attention to God's presence in our lives, whether at the time or in retrospect, have an obligation to share the stories we glean from those experiences. As we share our stories, we also try to draw out the stories of others, to help them recognize God in their lives, in the simple or complex tangibles of their day-to-day worlds.

The sermon well preached is designed to meet and love the listener where he or she is, and to gently (although sometimes not so gently) move that person to a deeper understanding of God. As we prepare to share our stories in a sermon or homily, we can look for insights into the ways of God by using a good Bible commentary and by paying attention to the historical, cultural, and literary aspects of the day's readings. In sharing our stories in the context of the day's lessons, we also need to make real connections for the listeners. We want them to find in our message something they can take into their hearts, using its wisdom to illuminate their lives, and so we take into consideration their lives, culture, and understandings. The stories in our sermons should challenge us and our listeners with the very radical love that is at the heart of God; the stories should, in short, proclaim the Good News.

LORD, open our lips. And our mouth shall proclaim your praise.
(BCP, 80)

Thus we may begin Daily Morning Prayer, or we may choose a sentence from Scripture appropriate to the season. When we first encounter Morning Prayer, we may be overwhelmed by the choices and the myriad rubrics (those italicized instructions for using the prayer book). With the renewed centrality of the Eucharist in Episcopal churches, Morning and Evening Prayer have become services that are foreign to many people. The officiant often must walk the congregation through the service when the congregation first encounters it or when the members encounter it infrequently. In Morning Prayer the familiar pattern of the Eucharist is replaced by one that sets the confession near the beginning and emphasizes many scriptural and ancient readings. The psalm for the day comes before the readings, not between them as in the Eucharist. Unless the church provides a congregation with opportunities to practice the daily offices, many Episcopalians are uncomfortable with the occasional use of them.

In helping people become comfortable with Morning Prayer, I do an instructional Morning Prayer, one in which I share the options and rubrics with the congregation, pointing out the appropriate choices for the particular day. I do this as unobtrusively as possible, limiting my comments to simple directions when possible. For example, I will say, "We follow this reading by reciting the canticle found on page 90, 'A Song of Praise.'" When I have a service for young people, I explain further what the rubrics are, what they mean, and the choices we have within the given instructions.

I always go to a service that I am to lead having read through it the night before and having already chosen appropriate sentences, canticles, and prayers for the day, depending on the season and Scripture readings. I mark these with sticky notes and add other directions as needed. This preparation increases my comfort level, and I hope that of the congregation as well. I also let the beauty and the pattern of the services reassure the people gathered.

The daily offices provide themes and motifs that repeat and build on themselves throughout each service. Our hymns add to and underscore the readings for the day; careful choosing of sentences and canticles will further enhance this feeling of order amidst chaos. Some people find messages in songs, some in psalms, some in the specific colors of church decorations, some in the homily, some in the canticles, and some in the prayers. The built-in redundancy should not become intrusive but remain suggestive of God's order and beauty in our world and of the power of God to enter into our lives. Each new presentation of an idea should build on the other, weaving God's love into our minds and hearts, reminding us that we are beloved, that we are called to love God, one another, and ourselves, and that we are called to sanctify our days to the Lord and to do all that we do in service to God and our companions, those we know and those we don't.

Morning Prayer invites us into a worship that centers on Scripture readings with which we hope our congregations become familiar. We are fed by the Word, nourished by prayers shared with the many who have gone before us, and sustained by the calling that we are all to minister to one another. In order for us to find these things in our daily offices, we need to be able to recognize their presence and to share that presence with others as they too participate in the services.

*Glorify the L*ORD*, all you works of the L*ORD*.*

(BCP, 88)

My primary reasons for reading Morning Prayer are to sanctify my day to the Lord and to center myself in the love of God and the traditions of the church.

I truly enjoy the predictability and expansiveness of Morning Prayer. It follows the same basic pattern: We are invited into the presence of the Lord; we confess our sins; and we move through the psalms, readings, praises, prayers, and thanksgivings. If we pray this service regularly, we know the routine and are comforted by it. Yet, as with all good order, Morning Prayer allows a great deal of freedom. The use of the canticles, which range over the realm of human emotions and needs, creates this freedom. Confined to their place in the structure, they nonetheless provide us with great choice and expression. There is Mary's "Yes, Lord," Simeon's freedom, Manasseh's penitence, Isaiah's trust in the Lord. In "A Song of Creation," the Three Young Men invoke all of God's world to glorify the Lord.

I try to begin my days with Morning Prayer, reading it by myself but

Meditations for Lay Readers – 45

preparing as though for public worship. I also try to pay attention to the seasons and read appropriate canticles. In order to simplify my life, I choose the sentences and canticles ahead of time, marking them with sticky notes. Then I use the Daily Office Lectionary or the Sunday Lectionary to find the psalms and readings for the day. I write them on sticky notes and mark their places in the Bible.

With the books marked, I take my place at my writing table; it is an old table at which my grandfather wrote sermons. Littered with my papers and books, it is now a sacred place at which I choose to pray when I am alone. I read Morning Prayer out loud, using the time to practice the cadence of the service and to reflect and listen. The spaces in between passages and the major sections provide times when I can simply listen to God, feeling present to God. Our services do not shy away from silence, finding no awkwardness there, but only peace. My dog often comes to listen to the service, finding some comfort in the strength of the words and the now familiar rhythms. He too is part of creation, an example of God's love, and so I remind him to glorify the Lord, taking my lead from the invocation for "A Song of Creation."

I keep a journal nearby and, if something seems particularly strong, I may pause to write it down. Sometimes these notes are used in meditations, sermons, and essays. Or they may be used simply for my later reflection, leading me into a different understanding of God, people, a situation, or me. I don't find journaling to be intrusive as I just jot down a few words to help me remember and, in doing so, offer myself to God's will, knowing that God often speaks to me through my writing and through the discipline of a structured prayer life. This discipline encircles me in God's word and encourages me to sanctify my day.

Worship and study support my ministry as a lay reader; they keep me centered in God, focused on God's order in creation, and open to the heart of the sacred.

The love of God has been poured into our hearts through the Holy Spirit that has been given to us. Thanks be to God.
(Romans 5:5; BCP, 105)

An Order of Service for Noonday offers the officiant and people a time out from a hectic day, a time to quiet ourselves to hear the Word of the Lord. When alone, I often use the service to remind me of Christ's love and sacrifice; the noonday service tells us that it was at noon that Christ stretched out his arms on the cross. Lay readers can use the noonday service as a way to stretch out our arms to the community, inviting the people into a loving prayer service where the Word of God feeds and soothes in the midst of the day.

The collects point to God's presence in our lives. We are to be representatives of God's radiance as we go out into the world, making disciples and bringing people into relationships with the Lord. Each of us is called to serve within the loving circle of God's arms and within the power of the Holy Spirit.

In this service we find the comforting words "Lord, have mercy. Christ, have mercy. Lord, have mercy." Repeating these, we are stronger, for we have acknowledged God's power in our lives; we know from where our strength comes. We are always empowered when we put ourselves in God's charge, knowing that God sends the Holy Spirit to comfort and direct us according to God's direction for us. The noonday service lets us take the time to hear that direction and to gain strength in order to follow it.

Your word is a lantern to my feet and a light upon my path.
(Psalm 119:105; BCP, 103)

Sometimes, when the timing is right, or when one of us needs the community gathered to pray, my office stops at noon and offers an Order of Service for Noonday. It is a rich time, a time when we acknowledge our common beliefs and our dedication to the church, God, and each other. We gather deliberately, taking turns leading the service, sometimes reading Scripture from the Daily Office and sometimes pausing to study and reflect on that reading, offering an impromptu meditation that builds as each of us comments or reflects on what has been read and said.

It is a good time, a time of putting aside the day's work and reaching into ourselves for our life work, for surely we are here to love God, one another, and ourselves. In pausing during the day, we offer time to praise God, to recognize God's will in our life. We pause and tell each other through the psalms, prayers, and intercessions that we care deeply for one another. We pause and offer ourselves to God's mercy, reminding ourselves of God's great and vast love for us. We leave the prayers knowing that we are loved for who we are, knowing that we can trust that great gift to us.

We offer the service when one of us feels fragile or under stress. We pray the prayers in joy when laughter fills us. We pray them in sorrow as we think of people's suffering. It is my prayer that each time I read the noonday service I will leave it taking something of God's light and Word with me, and that in moving through the rest of my day I will bring that light and Word into someone else's life.

Keep watch, dear LORD, with those who work, or watch, or weep this night, and give your angels charge over those who sleep.
(BCP, 124)

It was the joke of the summer camp: If I did Evening Prayer, I would always include the prayer that begins with these words. I have kept watch at night when weeping and praying seemed the only thing to do. I remember long nights when I would sleep on the floor next to my coughing and feverish son so that I could doze but wouldn't fall into a sleep so deep that I wouldn't awaken if he needed me. I remember the vigil at my father's side as he was dying. I remember times my mother has been sick and a long way from me. And I remember how, on one evening service when I prayed this prayer, the prayer reached a friend of mine whose husband is a policeman who works the graveyard shift. She thanked me again and again for praying for those whose nights are long and filled with potential danger.

Growing up in the Episcopal Church, I was rarely comfortable with extemporaneous prayer. For years I have carried a prayer book with me when I travel. To this day it takes great courage for me to pray out loud when the prayer is not written out. For me the poetry of the prayers found in the prayer book is often enough to calm a troubled mind. The repeating *w* sound in the "Keep watch" prayer strengthens the feeling that I am in an ordered world with a God who can create beauty out of chaos. To a mother, frightened to hear her child struggling to breathe in the night, the repetition of this simple prayer was a saving grace. Surely Jesus watching with us is one of the graces we receive, undeserved, from our God.

These words have kept me from despair. They are etched in my mind, a mantra to remind me, as the psalmist says, that "God is our refuge and strength, a very present help in trouble" (Psalm 46:1). Yes and Amen. God is truly a very present help in trouble. We are graced by God's presence. We imagine Jesus watching with us through a long night and suddenly we are not alone; the room is filled with a calmness that allows us to bear what must be borne. God's presence does not shield us from the pain, but rather it allows us to go through the pain, learning on the way how to invite Jesus to watch with us so that the burden is lighter and the lesson of love more easily learned.

Jesus said, "I am the light of the world; whoever follows me will not walk in darkness, but will have the light of life."

(BCP, 116)

Evening Prayer offers the light of the Word to a world that is becoming dark. In a very primitive sense, it acknowledges our fear of the dark and moves us into a right relationship with the dark through our understanding of and commitment to Christ: We have nothing to fear in the dark.

Evening Prayer can carry many of us beyond the service and into the awesome presence of God. Starting with the opening sentence, we acknowledge our receptiveness to the Word. Confessing, we empty ourselves into the heart of God, knowing that God's grace and our repentance will allow peace to settle among us. Invited into the soul of the Word, we hear the readings of ancient callings, psalms, and the gospel. The creed brings to us our beliefs. And then we pray, drawing on the prayer of Jesus, moving to petitions for ourselves and others, choosing carefully the collects that will touch the needs of the night. Knowing that all of us desire comforting, we pray for the mission of the church and for those who work and those who weep. A thanksgiving follows. We have much for which to be thankful. Gathered together or alone in the presence of the Lord and of the saints, past and present, we have traveled from a place of potential fear to a place of solace, peace, and quiet joy. Blessing the Lord, we move into the night with words of encouragement. We have been reminded that ours is a God of grace, of hope, of power.

When the services of a priest cannot be obtained, a deacon or lay reader may preside at the service.

(BCP, 490)

The rubrics for a burial service in The Book of Common Prayer allow for it to be led by laity. What an incredible privilege this is, to help the faithful on to the next part of their lives, to help those who mourn find comfort in the love of Christ Jesus. I've not had to lead a burial service, but I have been the lector at several, including my father's funeral. There was an audible gasp as I went forward to the podium. But I considered it an honor to read those words to the family and friends of this faithful churchman whose life had been one of pain and love.

I also considered it an honor to read at the funeral of the treasurer of our small church. The treasurer had been a gemologist; he took great pride in his beautiful minerals and in his artistry as a goldsmith and jeweler. The priest chose a lovely piece from Scripture that was full of the names of minerals. In this church filled with others interested in minerals and gemstones, I read from a carefully marked photocopy of the reading. I had phonetically written out each name, using a dictionary to get the names right. The poetry of the reading, with its vivid images and dancing gem names, brought close to home this man's belief in God the creator and redeemer. He lived in the liturgy, for ours is a liturgy of life, of perpetual light, of celebration, of resurrection.

I learned from the wonderful priest of this funeral how to create a liturgy from the life of the faithful, how to see in each person's life the gospel of our Lord, and how to remind us that God sees us each as individuals, counting the hairs on our head and seeing our passions and sorrows. The service points to God, who is all powerful and all loving, but it also points to the witness of the faithful departed. And where one can pull in hymns, readings, and a homily that illustrate the witness of the departed, one can create a testimony to the Lord our God.

Some of the church's oldest prayers appear in our burial service; they evoke in us the passing of time and the understanding of the communion of saints. The prayers express our joy as we note the passage of a loved one into "a nearer presence of our Lord," while at the same time they hold out our pain to the comfort that comes from a grief shared. It is an honor and a privilege to read or to officiate at a burial service: It demands our creativity and our faithfulness, our tears and our joy, and our understanding that nothing can separate us from the love of Christ Jesus.

Almighty God, Father of mercies and giver of comfort: Deal gra-
ciously, we pray, with all who mourn; that, casting all their care
on you, they may know the consolation of your love; through Jesus
Christ our LORD. Amen.

(BCP, 505)

Life sometimes gives us more than we can handle, and it is by God's
gracious love that we overcome the tragedies, crises, losses, and fears.
Standing over my father's body, we pray, knowing that he has just a few
more labored breaths and then he will be in pain no more. We have held
our simple vigil, a night of praying from the prayer book. A night of
nursing, loving, and crying. We know we are ready to let go; we know
the time has come. My sister is with him at the moment of his death; it
takes only a few more minutes for us to gather. The woman from hos-
pice encourages us to continue talking to him as we await the priest and
the doctor. It is a powerful moment. God is very present to us.

Into this scenario any one of us may be called. We may be the friend
who hears the news long distance; we may be the lector who must swal-

low tears and prepare to read the lessons at the funeral of a friend; we may be the lay reader called in the absence of a priest or deacon to officiate at the funeral. We must face our own understandings of death, our own patterns of grief, and our own abilities to support and walk with others who grieve. In doing so, it helps to read through the burial services and "An Order for Burial" in The Book of Common Prayer. For here we find our ancient fear of death held in the loving arms of Jesus. We are reminded that Jesus comforted Martha and Mary and that he wept for Lazarus. Our God understands our grief at losing to our immediate lives the life of a loved one.

In the prayer book, we find our needs for love and care acknowledged; those who mourn hear the prayers for them as well as for the deceased. And above all we find the reassurance that we are an Easter people, that our "liturgy for the dead is an Easter liturgy." God raised Jesus from the dead and so God will raise us and our beloved. Even in the midst of somber Lent, our liturgy is an Easter celebration and Easter hymns are appropriate. Jesus, raised from the dead, overcomes death for us; he overcomes the evil in our lives that would siphon off our life energy. And so we are reminded that the deceased will be raised up and that our lives are postresurrection lives with Christ Jesus' sacrifice there between us and the death of turning from life. We are reminded in the funeral liturgy that we are "alive in the Lord." Alleluia.

I lie down in peace; at once I fall asleep; for only you, LORD, make me dwell in safety.

(Psalm 4:8)

How many times have we gone to bed only to find the day's worries tweaking our minds? We find ourselves watching the clock, noting the slow passing of time while the demons of self-pity, fear, and anger play around with our thoughts. We find ourselves acknowledging the severity of a situation—a sick child, a dying parent, a budget that doesn't stretch nearly enough, a rocky relationship—and we stay awake watching the day's dangers unravel in front of us. Life is not easy, and no amount of magic thinking at the end of the day will produce peace. Yet there is a way to peace so that we can sleep.

The prayers of the church, especially the prayers of Compline, recognize the feverish activities of the day, the roaring lion who brings the demons of self-doubt, the weariness of the "changes and the chances of this life." But all of these burdens are lightened by a God who says "Come to me... I will give you rest." We are called by these prayers to invite God into our lives, to have God join us as we sort out our day and ask God's protection for us. We are called by these prayers to invite God in at the same time as we move toward God. It is in this opening up, in this trusting, that we will find peace.

We are to hand God the troubles of the day, to let them rest within God's changeless love, and to trust that in the end all will be well. God knows this isn't easy for us. Scripture tells of the struggles of many, including Jesus. And yet there is always the lifting up, the joy that comes from knowing that one is beloved of God. In that love we can sleep, dwelling in the safety that is the Lord.

...let your holy angels dwell with us to preserve us in peace.
(BCP, 133)

When I was a child I had a glow-in-the-dark, plastic drinking glass next to my bed. It had a picture of Jesus on it. I also had a blanket with which I slept. Most of the time I needed it tucked over my neck as I slept on my stomach. I can still feel the warm, secure feeling of that soft wool and the comfort that the yellow glow of the glass gave me. It is hard as an adult to recapture that feeling of absolute safety. The day's dangers drift into my dreams, taking on all sorts of bizarre attitudes. The demons of self-doubt and of self-pity join hands with those of fear and anger. These demons poke and prod me, preventing me from sleeping.

The writers of the prayers and Scripture that make up Compline know the awful things that can beset a person at bedtime. We are told to "be sober, be watchful; your adversary the devil prowls around like a roaring lion" (1 Peter 5:8–9a). Certainly that lion of fear and distrust has prowled through my bedroom many times. The prayers speak of the "changes and chances of this life," acknowledging the often capricious things that can happen to us when we have other plans. The prayers speak of the "snares of the enemy," and certainly many of us have made enemies as we have spoken for Christ's ministry in this world, or have lived our lives while trying to be true to God's image for us.

But the prayers always offer the love of God to us: the protection from our own fears when we know we are loved. We are told to be firm in our faith, to resist the lion's fear-ridden prowling, to hand over to God our burdens so that God can make them light. We are told it is okay to acknowledge our pain and our fear, but in doing so we must acknowledge God's ability to offer security and safety. The Creator gives us love and we are to trust that love, knowing that it is offered unconditionally.

It is hard to trust that love, to trust that ultimately we will be okay, but that is what God calls us to do. The prayers of Compline offer us a chance to invite God into our lives, to admit our fears, and to hand them over to God. The prayers do not invite us to go it alone, ignore God's love, or take our lives solely into our own hands. No, we are to lift our hands in the blessing of God and in the giving over of our troubles to God. We are to trust with all that we have. We are to rest in the absolute security of knowing that regardless of all else we are loved beyond anything we can imagine. And so we are called to dwell among the holy angels who preserve us in peace.

Prayers

Sunday Morning
Dear God,
If I am to lead the service this morning, let me lead well. If I am to read this morning, let your voice be heard through mine. If I am to sit among the congregation, let my prayers be both inward and outward, listening always for your will and upholding others and myself to your undying love.

In Christ's name,
Amen

Sunday Evening

Dear God,

The work of today is done; thank you for guiding me through the day. As I move from a day of lessons, coffee hours, services, and the business of the church, let me remember this evening that your resurrection brings us into new life with you. As I gather my memories of today, its ups and downs, let me hand them to you for your care and guidance. Help me to seek your will as I continue to serve your church.

In Christ's name,
Amen

Monday Morning
Dear God,
It is the beginning of the week in the secular world. Help me to see your face in each person I meet, to carry my servant ministry from the church to the world. Help me to find your way in each challenge I face, pausing often during the day to give thanks for your presence in my life, the people who bless my day, and the gifts I bring to my family and friends.

In Christ's name,
Amen

Monday Evening

Dear God,

The day is quieting. I hurried perhaps a bit too much, anxious about results, forgetting for a time to enjoy the moment. I may have snapped at someone in my haste, been all too human as I played over and over in my mind the happenings of the day. But I felt your presence Lord, saw it in the smile of acquaintances, heard it in the laughter of children, watched it in the plume behind a jet. I found comfort in knowing that you have gone before me, waited for me, and watched with me. For your presence in my day, I am thankful.

In Christ's name,
Amen

Tuesday Morning
Dear God,
Today I offer myself as a sacrifice to you, wanting to do your will, wanting to serve your people. Grant me the patience to listen, the right mind to think, the courage to speak, and the wisdom to love. Help me to show people the love of your Son, letting those who need to care for me do so, allowing those who offer hospitality the benefit of my smile and gratitude. Help me to care for those who ask and to notice those who don't. Let me be ever mindful of the needs of others.

In Christ's name,
Amen

Tuesday Evening
Dear God,
It is good that there is darkness into which we can sink and rest, knowing that we are in your presence. It is good to close the day in prayer and deep communion with you. It is good to find thanks for each small thing of the day. It is good to go slowly to sleep, remembering our Lord's prayer to you, remembering that you offer more than food—you offer the very essence of life. It is good to chase away the demons of the day, knowing that your will is for our healing and not our destruction.

In Christ's name,
Amen

Wednesday Morning
Dear God,
You tell us to love our neighbors as ourselves; help me then to love myself today. Let me seek joy where I can and celebrate my lay ministry among your people. Remind me to get some exercise, to take time just to be with you, to eat well, and to honor your being in everything I do. Encourage me to be patient with my mistakes, to learn from them, and in doing so to move into the kingdom that is here and now.

In Christ's name,
Amen

Wednesday Evening
Dear God,
This morning I asked your help in loving myself; tonight I ask your help in loving my fellow lay readers, those who are close by and those who are far from me. I ask that each of their acts of ministry reach many people. May you walk with them in the challenges they face as they strive to bring your Word to your people. May you sit with them as they pray for guidance. I ask that you be with them as they discern how best to use their many talents in the church, without losing sight of their own needs and those of their families and friends. Lord, bless their studies, that their insights may be of you.

In Christ's name,
Amen

Thursday Morning
Dear God,
Thank you for today, for another chance to move among your people, and for another chance to celebrate your life in mine and in those whose paths I cross. Thank you for service in your church, for the ability to read the lessons and lead Morning or Evening Prayer, and for the quiet time of Compline, with its cadence of calmness, as I enter into the dark hours of the night. I thank you for the richness of the Daily Office readings. For the prayers that I pray together with Christians around the world and for a community from which to reach out to the world at large, thank you.

In Christ's name,
Amen

Thursday Evening
Dear God,
Tonight, as I prepare to quiet my life, slow down, and listen in the still-ness for your Word, be with the ministers of your church. Reassure them of your love, regardless of the stresses they face and the successes or fail-ures they perceive in their lives. Remind them that they are each loved by you, that you go before them to open doors into those very places they long to be. Show them that through your Son all shall be well. Reassure them that it is their "Here I am, Lord," not their perfection, for which you ask. Help us each to humbly serve you, knowing we are loved.

In Christ's name,
Amen

Friday Morning
Dear God,
On this morning your servant Mary wept, knowing that her son would soon die. She met that as courageously as she met his awesome birth, knowing that in serving you she could suffer all things because the kingdom was in her heart as she answered "Yes, Lord." It is not always easy to serve you, Lord; people mock us; throw phrases at us, as though we were lower than they; hold us up for public scrutiny, trying to find our faults on which to hang their criticism. Yet, like Mary, we can hold fast to knowing that your will is one of love—a love that endures all things. Be with your servants, Lord. Hold us in our pain, smile with us in our joy.

In Christ's name,
Amen

Friday Evening

Dear God,

How dark that Friday evening must have seemed as Jesus' body was put into the tomb. His disciples, some having to live with the guilt of having turned from him, mourned at their terrible loss, not knowing that in a few days God's love would release him from the tomb. Help us, as we sometimes falter in our faith, to remember that your love will release us from our tomb of despair. Encourage us as we serve through the dark times, when all seems blank and decaying. Comfort us when our ability to pray and trust falters. Be our strength through our bleak nights, and let the love of your Son make us alive again.

In Christ's name,
Amen

Saturday Morning
Dear God,
As I go over the lessons for tomorrow and meditate on your Word, let me hear and do your will. May my understandings of Scripture, tradition, and reason be of value to those who hear them, and may they honor you. Let me look anew at the familiar words of the prayer book; help them create in me a heart open to reconciliation, a mind open to new opportunities to serve you, and a body willing to savor the beauties of your day and the dancing of your words.

In Christ's name,
Amen

Saturday Evening
Dear God,
Tomorrow is your feast day, a day of celebration, a day of wonder as we again remind ourselves that in gathering together we become more fully the body of Christ. As we receive nourishment through the bread and wine, and through the Word, let us seek your will so that when we move from the body gathered into a world that is scattered we may be ministers to all your people, offering the refuge of understanding and compassion to those in need. We are all in need, Lord; keep us mindful that we each need the celebration of life that is your Son, and that we each need to serve as best as we can where we are sent. For the ministry of lay reading, I am most grateful, Lord; make me an instrument of peace within and outside the church.

In Christ's name,
Amen